Scary Creatures
of the
NIGHT

Written by
John Malam

FRANKLIN WATTS
An Imprint of Scholastic Inc.
NEW YORK • TORONTO • LONDON • AUCKLAND • SYDNEY
MEXICO CITY • NEW DELHI • HONG KONG
DANBURY, CONNECTICUT

Created and designed
by David Salariya

Long-eared owl

Author:

John Malam studied ancient history and
archaeology at the University of Birmingham,
England, and then worked as an archaeologist at
the Ironbridge Gorge Museum in Shropshire. He is
now an author specializing in nonfiction books for
children on a wide range of subjects. He lives in
Cheshire with his wife and their two young
children. Website: www.johnmalam.co.uk

Artists:

John Francis
Robert Morton
Carolyn Scrace
Bob Hersey
Lizzie Harper
Mark Bergin

Series Creator:

David Salariya was born in Dundee,
Scotland. In 1989 he established The Salariya Book
Company. He has illustrated a wide range of books
and has created many new series for publishers in the
U.K. and overseas. He lives in Brighton with his wife,
illustrator Shirley Willis, and their son.

Editor: Stephen Haynes

Editorial Assistants:
Rob Walker, Tanya Kant

Picture Research:
Mark Bergin, Carolyn Franklin

Photo Credits:

ANT Photo Library/NHPA: 9
Cadmium: 10, 14, 22, 23
Gerry Cambridge/NHPA: 29
Corbis: 5
Ingram Publishing: 24
John Foxx Images: 11

Created, designed, and produced by
The Salariya Book Company Ltd
Book House
25 Marlborough Place
Brighton BN1 1UB

A CIP catalog record for this title is available
from the Library of Congress.

ISBN-13: 978-0-531-20424-5 (Lib. Bdg.)
978-0-531-21009-3 (Pbk.)
ISBN-10: 0-531-20424-3 (Lib. Bdg.)
0-531-21009-X (Pbk.)

Published in the United States by Franklin Watts
An Imprint of Scholastic Inc.
557 Broadway
New York, NY 10012

Printed in China.

PAPER FROM

SUSTAINABLE
FORESTS

Contents

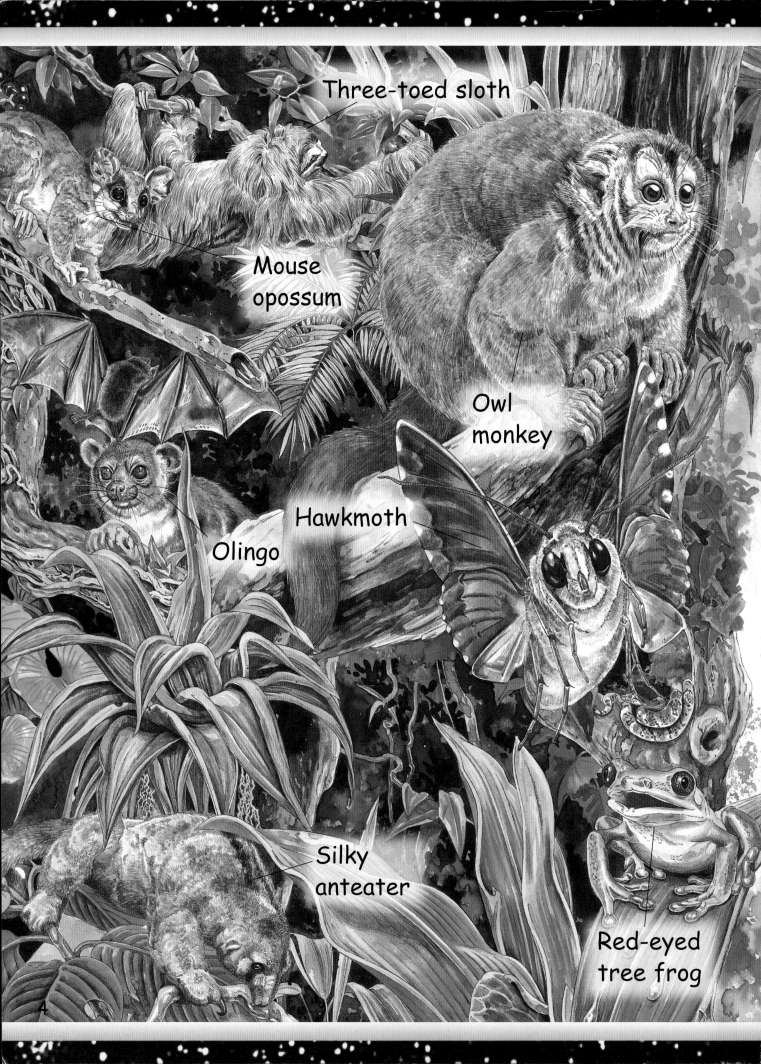

Three-toed sloth

Mouse opossum

Owl monkey

Olingo

Hawkmoth

Silky anteater

Red-eyed tree frog

What Are Night Creatures?

When the sun goes down, it's time for many animals to wake up. As daylight fades, out come bats, boa constrictors, spiders, owls, and leopards. These are **nocturnal** animals. They sleep in the day and become active at night. Darkness is when these animals see best and feed best. Nocturnal animals have learned to live in the dark, and they have developed ways of making the most of nighttime.

Most owls are night hunters. They have big eyes that are extremely sensitive to light. An owl can see its **prey** in very low light and swoops in quickly and quietly.

Many nocturnal animals, from tiny frogs to large mammals, live in the **tropical** rain forest of South America. The picture opposite shows just a few of them.

 Did You Know?

Guinea pigs, rabbits, foxes, moths, and beetles are called **crepuscular** (twilight) animals. They are active at dawn, before it is too light; and at dusk, before it is too dark.

5

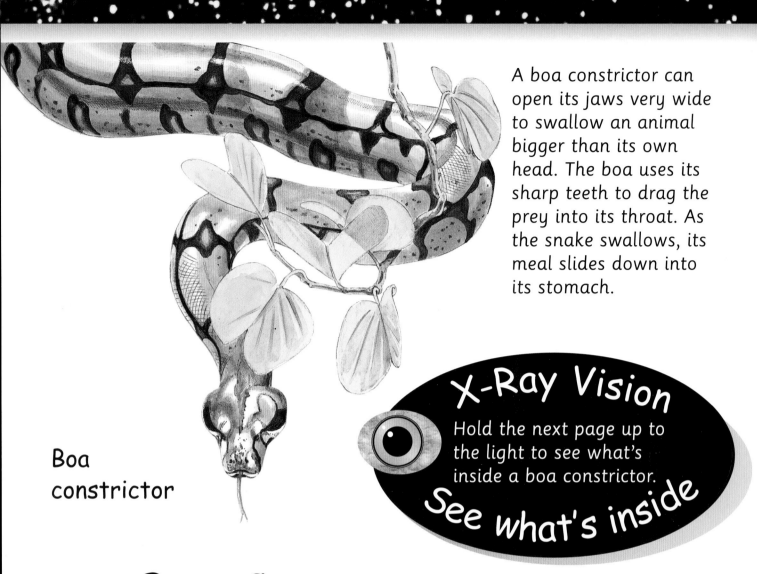

A boa constrictor can open its jaws very wide to swallow an animal bigger than its own head. The boa uses its sharp teeth to drag the prey into its throat. As the snake swallows, its meal slides down into its stomach.

Boa constrictor

X-Ray Vision

Hold the next page up to the light to see what's inside a boa constrictor.

See what's inside

Are Boa Constrictors Strong?

Yes! Boa constrictors are big, strong snakes that live in the deserts, grasslands, and forests of South and Central America. They live on the ground and in trees, and they hunt at night. Boas eat lizards, bats, birds, rats, monkeys, and squirrels, which they kill by **constriction**. They twist tightly around their prey, choke them to death, then swallow their bodies whole, head first.

Full stomach

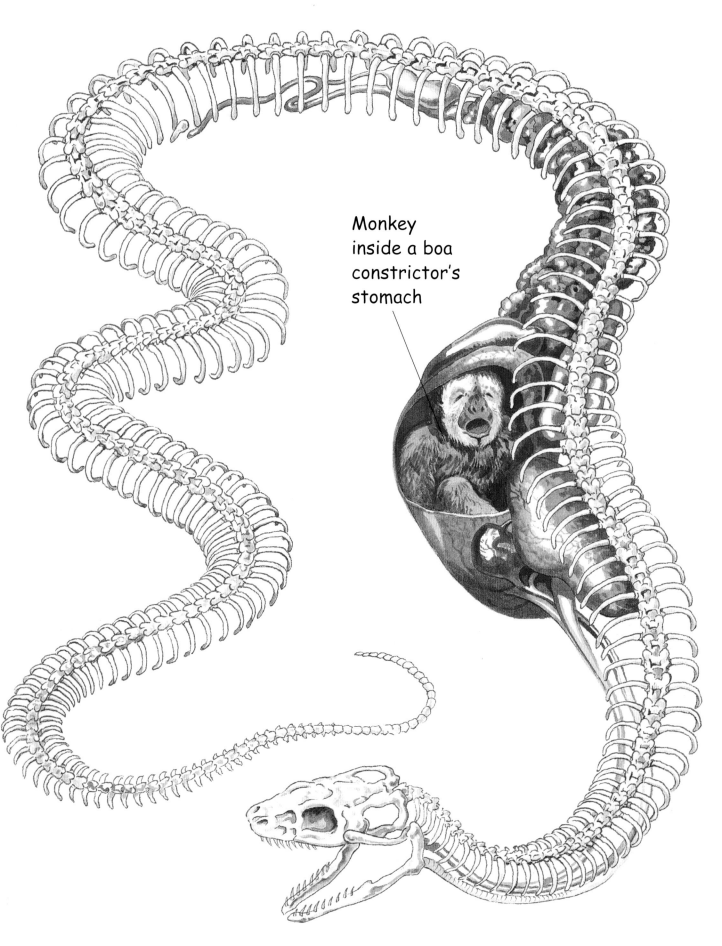

Monkey inside a boa constrictor's stomach

What Do Night Animals Do in the Day?

After being awake and active during the night, nocturnal animals use the daytime to rest and recover. Owls roost in old buildings and trees, tarantula spiders return to their burrows, and mice huddle together in cozy nests. All keep very still so that **predators** will not find them.

Bats live together in groups called **colonies**. In the daytime, a colony rests inside a cave, a tunnel, or the roof of a building. Hundreds or thousands of bats may hang there, all resting together until night comes.

Did You Know?

Some night animals need a lot of sleep. The giant armadillo snoozes for eighteen hours a day.

Long-eared bat

Why Do Big Cats Hunt at Night?

Many big cats are nocturnal, including lions, tigers, and leopards. They rest in the day, saving their energy until dark. At night, cats' eyes gather as much light as possible. Light enters through their large pupils and is reflected off a layer at the back of the eye called the **tapetum**. All cats have good night vision and hunt at night, when they can sneak up on their prey without being seen.

Serval

The serval is a small cat with a big bite. It is most active at dawn and dusk, but some are wide awake at night. It hunts rats, hares, snakes, and lizards.

Indian tiger

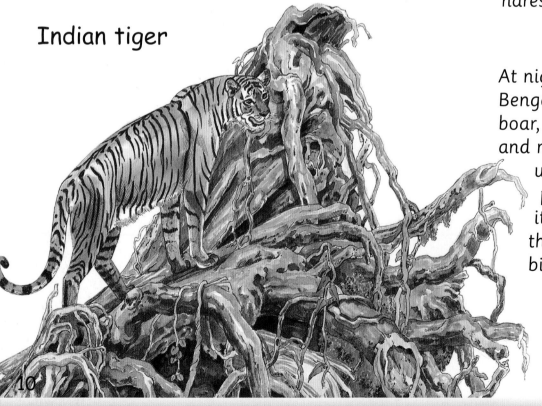

At night the Indian, or Bengal, tiger hunts wild boar, water buffalo, deer, and monkeys. It creeps up on its prey, pounces on it, drags it to the ground, and then kills it with a bite to the neck.

Did You Know?

The jaguar is a big cat found mostly in South and Central America. Some say that its name means "the beast that kills with one leap."

Jaguar

What Lives in the Rain Forest at Night?

Tropical rain forests around the world are home to a great variety of night animals. When darkness arrives, these creatures emerge from their daytime resting places. Snakes slither in silence, insects crawl and fly, and mammals creep and leap. Nighttime is their active period—and the most dangerous time for them. As they search for food, their movements give them away. If a predator is watching, the hunter becomes the hunted!

Green tree python

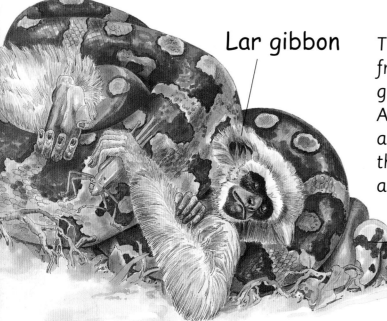

Lar gibbon

The Indian python is a massive snake from the tropical forests of Asia. A fully grown adult can be 20 feet (6 m) long. At night the python ambushes birds and mammals, wraps itself around them, and suffocates them until they are dead. Then it swallows them whole.

Indian python

The bigger the prey, the longer it takes the python to digest it. This gibbon will take a month to break down inside the python's stomach.

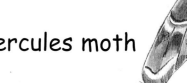

Hercules moth

These night animals live in the tropical rain forests of New Guinea and Australia.

Goodfellow's tree kangaroo

Did You Know?

The sugar glider is a possum which has a **membrane** of skin between its fingers and toes. When it jumps from a tree it spreads out the membrane and can glide for up to 165 feet (50 m) before landing in another tree.

Sugar glider

What Senses Are Useful at Night?

Nighttime animals have highly developed senses of sight, hearing, and smell. Unlike **diurnal** (daytime) animals, nocturnal animals such as cats and owls can see at night.

Some bats use hearing to find prey. They make high-pitched sounds that bounce off flying insects. Bats hear the echoes and then know where to find the prey. That's called **echolocation**.

Eurasian owl

At the back of an owl's eyes, the shiny layer called the tapetum works like a mirror. It reflects the faintest traces of light back into the owl's eyes, giving the owl excellent sight at night.

It's good to have big eyes. The bigger they are the better they are for seeing at night because they let more light in. At night the slow loris looks for insects to eat.

Slow loris

X-Ray Vision

Hold the next page up to the light to see the skeleton of the flying bat.

See what's inside

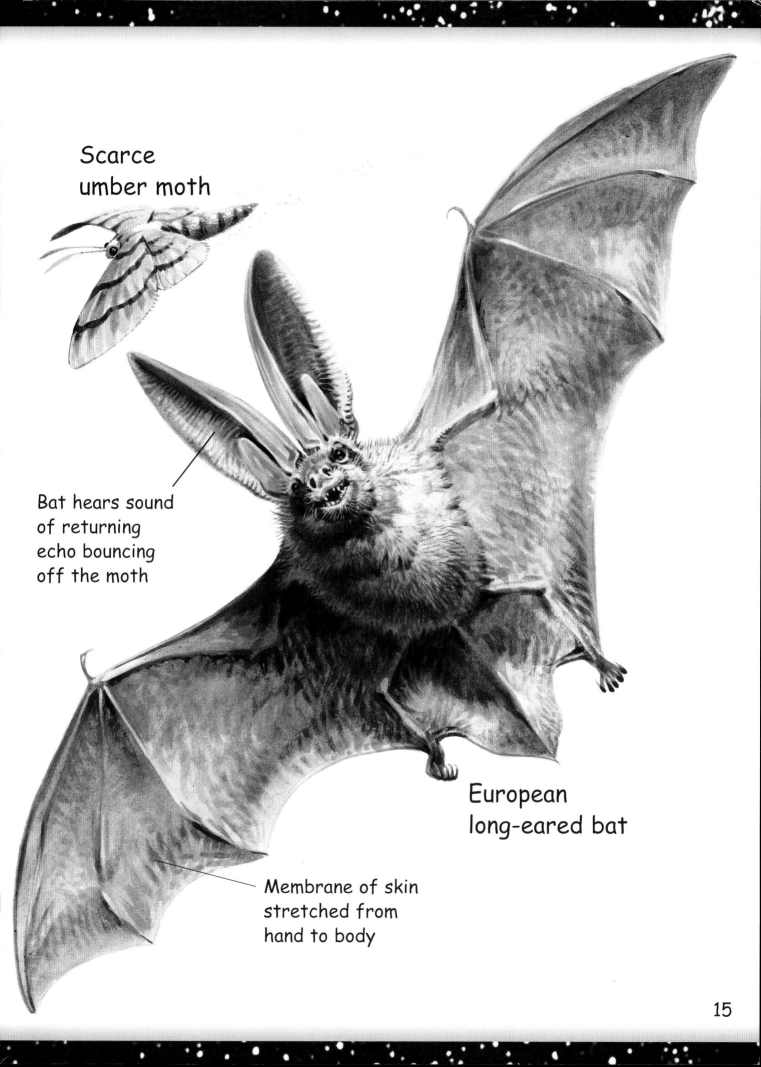

Scarce
umber moth

Bat hears sound
of returning
echo bouncing
off the moth

European
long-eared bat

Membrane of skin
stretched from
hand to body

15

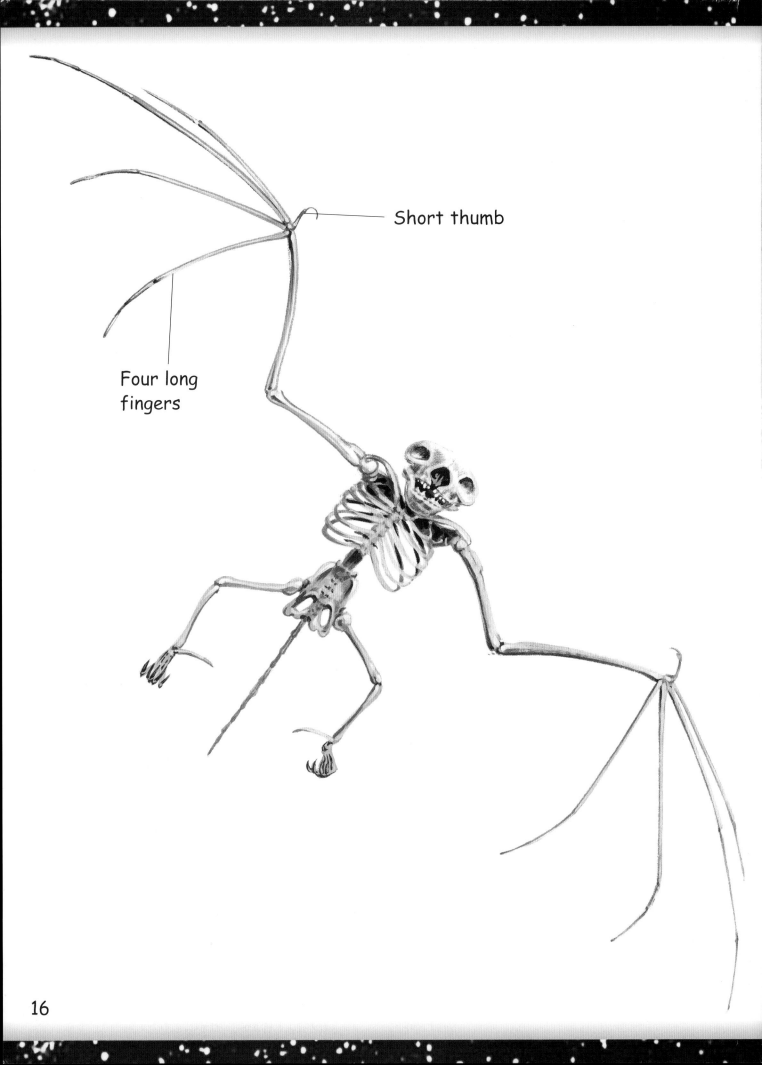

Short thumb

Four long
fingers

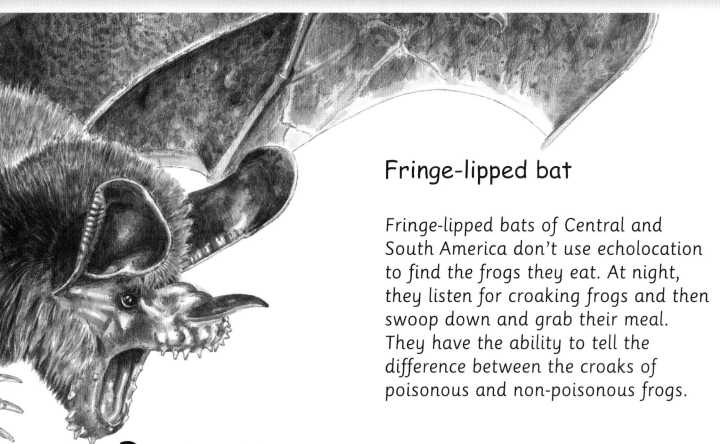

Fringe-lipped bat

Fringe-lipped bats of Central and South America don't use echolocation to find the frogs they eat. At night, they listen for croaking frogs and then swoop down and grab their meal. They have the ability to tell the difference between the croaks of poisonous and non-poisonous frogs.

Do Bats Suck Blood?

There are about one thousand different kinds of bats in the world. About two-thirds of all bats eat insects, and most others eat fruit, pollen, and **nectar**. However, one bat family doesn't eat insects or fruit. Instead, the vampire bats of South America feed on blood. At night, they land on cows or horses and bite through their skin. But vampire bats do not *suck* blood; they lick the flowing blood with their tongues.

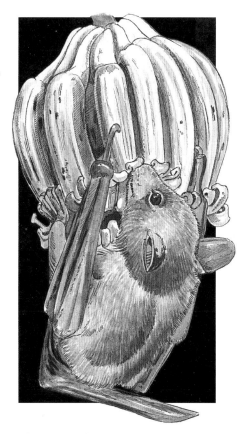

Fruit bat

Why Do Sea Turtles Come Onto Land?

The green turtle, a kind of sea turtle, spends most of its time swimming in the ocean. It's a big animal, and its flippers are designed for moving through water. But on land, these flippers are put to other uses. Females crawl onto sandy beaches at night and slowly haul themselves above the high-tide mark. Then, in a safe place, they use their back flippers to dig a deep hole in the sand. It's a nest where more than 100 eggs are laid. The turtle covers her nest with sand and then returns to the sea.

Female green turtle

Did You Know?

Green turtles have a good sense of direction. They often lay their eggs on the same beach where they themselves were born many years before.

Ghost crabs and frigate birds attack the baby turtles

The baby turtles hatch from their eggs after about 60 days. They hatch at night and crawl straight to the sea. Crabs and gulls attack them on the beach, and sharks and dolphins eat them in the water.

When a green turtle hatches from its egg it is only about 2 inches (50 mm) long. If it survives the dangerous walk to the sea—and if it escapes from the ocean's predators—it can expect to grow to 5 feet (1.5 m) long, and weigh about 300 pounds (135 kg). It might live for 80 years, and females will lay thousands of eggs in their lifetime.

Green turtle **hatchling**

What Lurks at the Bottom of the Sea?

The seabed is the daytime resting place of the angel shark. It lives in most oceans, hiding at the bottom of the sea under a layer of mud or sand. Only its bulging eyes poke above the seabed. The angel shark is an ambush predator. At night, it watches for squid and fish to come within grabbing distance. It jumps up, sucks in, swallows, and then settles back to lurk again.

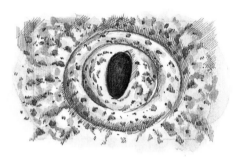

Angel shark's eye

The angel shark's eyes are very sensitive to light. Shiny tapetum cells inside its eyes make dim light seem bright, helping it to see clearly in the dark.

White-tip reef sharks

Like the angel shark, the white-tip reef shark is a nighttime feeder that dwells near the bottom of the sea. Found in the Indian and Pacific oceans, it rests throughout the day, hardly moving at all. When night arrives, it becomes active and starts to search for food.

The angel shark has a flat head and body. Its fins are large and wide. When it rests on the seabed it is almost invisible, because its coloring and speckles **camouflage** it against the sand.

Did You Know?

The angel shark, also known as the sand devil or monkfish, has a mouthful of sharp teeth. It has three rows of 20 teeth in its top jaw and 18 teeth in its bottom jaw.

Angel shark

White-tip reef sharks are the wolves of the sea. They hunt in large numbers, exploring crevices, holes, and caves in search of prey such as octopus, lobsters, crabs, eels, and other fish.

Why Do Owls Spin Their Heads?

Most birds have movable eyes on the sides of their heads. This gives them all-around vision. Owls have eyes in front and cannot move them, so they can see only straight ahead. To see to the side or behind, they must turn their heads. Owls can spin their heads in almost a full circle without moving their bodies.

When an owl sits on a branch, it keeps very still. It has an excellent sense of hearing, and when it hears a movement it turns its head to have a look. Because it doesn't turn its body at the same time, it doesn't draw attention to itself, so its prey isn't scared away.

Pair of barn owls

Did You Know?

The great horned owl does not have horns—and the long-eared owl does not have long ears, either! The long tufts on their heads are feathers that just happen to look like horns or ears.

Great horned owl

What Happens in Deserts at Night?

The world's sandy deserts are some of the hottest places on the planet. In the Sahara Desert, in Africa, temperatures reach a sweltering 122° Fahrenheit (50° C) during the day. It's too hot to be out in such extreme heat, so many desert animals rest in burrows and other sheltered places. At night, when the temperature is cooler, they emerge from their dens and shelters. They are then active in the hours of darkness.

Desert scorpion

Scorpions are desert predators that ambush their prey at night. They can sense movements in the dark, then grab beetles, spiders, and centipedes with their pincers.

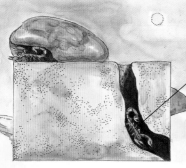

Scorpions seek shade during the day

Oasis

Did You Know?

A kangaroo rat can live its whole life without drinking a drop of liquid. All of the water it needs comes from the seeds it eats.

The fennec fox is the smallest member of the fox family, and like other foxes it is nocturnal. It lives in northern Africa, where it hunts rodents, insects, lizards, and birds. The fennec's very large ears have a double purpose. At night they help the fox hear prey, and in the day they help keep the fox cool by releasing body heat.

Nocturnal animals that live in hot deserts have adapted to their harsh environment. They have learned how to survive with little or no water. Desert mammals are often a light color, which reflects heat and keeps them cool.

Fennec fox

Gecko

Jerboa

Kangaroo rat

Could Dinosaurs See at Night?

Scientists think some dinosaurs were more active at night than in the daytime. Troodon,* a meat-eating dinosaur that lived near the North Pole, and Leaellynasaura,** a plant-eater that lived near the South Pole, had bigger eyes than most dinosaurs. Since they lived in places where nights were long and dark, night vision would have been essential to their survival.

* pronounced "TRO-a-don"
** "lee-ell-in-a-SORE-a"

Curled up tightly inside its egg is a baby Troodon. As an adult it grew to about 6.5 feet (2 m) long, with eyes about 2 inches (50 mm) across. It was a slender dinosaur that walked and ran on its two back legs. A **carnivore**, it preyed on smaller reptiles and mammals.

Inside a Troodon egg

Troodon

Saurornithoides

Troodon's eyes faced slightly forward, which is typical of animals that hunt at night. This helped it to judge distances, allowing it to pounce on its prey.

Why Do Creepy Crawlies Come Out at Night?

Nighttime is best for moths, spiders, and many kinds of insects because there are fewer predators around to bother them. If they came out in the day, they would be eaten by birds, frogs, and lizards. Under cover of darkness, moths sip nectar from flowers, other insects forage for food, and spiders wait for prey. Their senses work best at night, especially their sense of smell, which helps them sniff out food.

Cockroaches

Cockroaches hide during the day. At night they emerge in large numbers and eat just about anything.

Tarantula fangs

The Mexican red-kneed tarantula is a large, hairy spider from Central and South America. It lives in a burrow during the day. At night it waits by the entrance for passing insects, millipedes, scorpions, and other spiders. The tarantula jumps on its prey, killing it by injecting it with poison through its fangs.

Mexican red-kneed tarantula

Did You Know?

Moths are attracted to bright lights at night. They flutter around lightbulbs, spiraling up to the source of the light. They settle near the light because they think it's day, so it must be time to rest!

Emperor moth

Night Creature Facts

Aye-aye

The aye-aye, from Madagascar, is the world's largest nocturnal primate. It eats grubs that live inside trees. To find a grub, it taps on a tree trunk and listens for a hollow sound. Then it bites into the hollow, pokes its long, thin middle finger into the space, and picks out a fat, juicy grub.

The color of an owl's eyes tells the time of day when the owl is active. Owls with yellow eyes are diurnal hunters. Those with orange eyes are crepuscular hunters, while owls with dark eyes are nocturnal.

The eyes of nocturnal animals see mostly rough outlines and little or no color. They are big to attract maximum light at night. An owl's eyes fill over half of its skull.

In daylight, nocturnal animals such as lizards can narrow their pupils by squinting or closing their eyelids. This helps to keep bright light out of their sensitive eyes.

Twenty million Mexican free-tailed bats live in Bracken Cave, Texas. They eat an estimated 275 tons (250 metric tons) of insects every night!

The venom of a Mexican red-kneed tarantula paralyzes its prey and starts to dissolve it. Once the prey's insides have started to turn to liquid, the spider sucks it out, until all that is left is a hollow skin or a body case.

Asian leopard cat attacking a lesser tree shrew

Glossary

camouflage Special coloring that makes an animal difficult to see in its usual habitat.

carnivore A meat-eating animal.

colony A large family group of bats or other animals living together.

constriction The act of crushing by squeezing; snakes that kill their prey by crushing are called **constrictors**.

crepuscular Active mostly in twilight, at dusk and dawn.

diurnal Active mostly during the day.

echolocation The method used by bats to detect their prey. Bats make high-pitched sounds and listen for these sounds as they bounce back off the prey.

hatchling A newly hatched animal.

membrane A thin, tough layer of skin.

nectar A sugary substance produced by flowers to attract birds and insects, which then help to pollinate the flowers.

nocturnal Active mostly at night.

predator An animal that hunts and kills other animals for food.

prey An animal that is eaten or hunted by a predator.

tapetum (or **tapetum lucidum**) A layer of reflecting cells at the back of the eye of some animals. It helps them to see in the dark.

tropical Belonging to the tropics—the part of the earth farthest from the poles, where the temperature is always hot.

Mouse opossum

Index

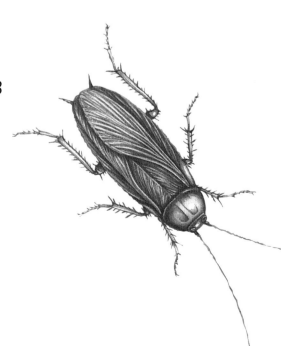